Openly

OBEDIENT

A *21* Day Diary & Devotional

For Living Your Faith Out Loud

Janelle A. Jones

Business Strategist: Rashida McKenzie

Editing and Book Consulting: ELOHAI International

Publishing & Media: www.ElohaiIntl.com

ISBN: 978-1-79-564907-0

Printed in the United States of America

Dedication

God, Thank you! You saved me from my past and turned me into who you wanted me to be.

To my amazing son Dallas, thank you for being the best son in the whole wide world. I want you to know, no matter how life goes, Jesus will always love you, and so will I. You have so much life ahead of you and I'm excited to witness your journey. Continue loving Jesus, praying for others, and believing you can be and do anything you put your mind to. Always remember how mighty God is. **I love you and I'm so glad Jesus put us together.**

To my uncle, Dr. Douglas Jones, God used you to plant a seed in my life. On different occasions, you asked, "Have you started writing your book?" All you saw were a few Facebook posts of me sharing my testimonies, but you saw something in me that I didn't see in myself. Thank you for always telling me "I'm so proud of you." That has meant so much. Thank you.

o·pen·ly

adverb

without concealment, deception, or prevarication, especially where these might be expected; frankly or honestly.

o·be·di·ent

noun

submission to another's authority.

"If you are willing and obedient, you will eat the good things of the land." - Isaiah 1:19

TABLE OF CONTENTS

Introduction

Being obedient isn't easy, but it's worth it. It's never too late to get on track. It doesn't matter what your past looks like, you can live an obedient life starting today, as soon as right now. God can turn your mess into a message and your test into a testimony. Whatever He is telling you to do, trust Him and believe it's His best! God wants to give you His best, but He has to know you're ready for it. He has a purpose for you but you have to seek Him daily to find that purpose. Believe me, He will tell you! And once you have that intimate encounter with Him, it will be something so amazing. The best for your life is still possible. You have to believe, be open, and help others live their best lives by sharing your story. Let someone else know how real God is so they too can grow a desire to know Him more.

This book is a personal diary that I'm sharing with others to show how God has used my past to make me the woman I am today. The book is a day-by-day story, and each day walks you through the highlights of my life from childhood to adulthood. It is designed to be a twenty-one day devotional which should help you spend three consecutive weeks with God by meditating on each scripture and reflecting on the "Faith Lessons" of each day. If you choose to read the book in a few days, I still encourage you to intentionally spend twenty-one days of meditating, reflecting and perhaps even journaling. A habit is formed in twenty-one days and it is my prayer that you continue to deepen your relationship with God.

For the next twenty-one days, I challenge you to seek God in new ways and watch Him do something new in your life. As He shows up in your life, be open and share your testimony with others.

Stay hidden in His word and keep trusting the process.

1. His Voice

Galatians 2:20

I have been crucified with Christ and I no longer live, but Christ lives in me. The life I now live in the body, I live by faith in the Son of God, who loved me and gave himself for me.

God, your voice woke me up with the idea for this book, and all I could do was lay there in awe. That has never happened to me before and it felt amazing. Thank you for the confirmation that gave me confidence to write this book.

I'm obeying you and doing what you instructed me to do. Writing this book is allowing me to show my obedience to you. To be open and tell the truth about what you've brought me through and how you intentionally used everything I went through to make me the person I am today. I've learned that spirituality can often be showed in secrecy. We don't share our struggles out of fear of being judged, talked about, and even ridiculed. From my deepest secrets to my past insecurities, I promise to give you all the praise, honor, and glory in my life. So this book is holding up my end of the promise.

Some things in this book will be shared for the first time with the people who mean the most to me.

I didn't want to do this because I feared being viewed differently by the people in my life that knows the "Janelle" I am today. However, as I started writing, you told me to be open. You told me I can't live in fear because I am fearfully and wonderfully made and that I am a child of the most high. You told me that my family and friends will continue loving me despite what I've overcome. You told me that no one is perfect and we all have a past. I am not who I used to be.

I've realized that being open with my testimonies has given hope to others and that's exactly what He wants us to do. We'll never know who we can help if we keep our stories to ourselves.

Faith Lesson:

Our life experiences are to be shared with others to help them get through their experiences too.

Today I will...

_____

_____

_____

_____

_____

_____

_____

_____

_____

_____

_____

_____

_____

_____

_____

_____

_____

_____

_____

_____

OPENLY OBEDIENT

2. Gratitude is an Attitude

Philippians 4:6

Do not be anxious about anything, but in every situation, by prayer and petition, with THANKSGIVING, present your requests to God.

Each day I wake up, I'm excited because I know I still have a purpose to fulfill. I start each day with a grateful heart. I thank God for bringing me to the very point I am in life every chance I get. I thank Him for the big things and the little things.

It's very important to have gratitude. Gratitude strengthens our emotions; it allows us to reduce the feelings of envy, makes our memories happier, and lets us experience good feelings. Give thanks for where you are right now because things could always be worse. I have experienced setbacks and thought of myself as a failure, but I've also seen God open doors that could only be from Him. I know firsthand how it feels to sit in a seat of favor that only God could orchestrate. Be thankful for the open doors and closed doors that you've experienced in life. There's a reason behind it all.

If we are not thankful for what we have, why should He give us something else to grumble about? When God sees that we genuinely appreciate and are thankful for the big and little things, He will bless us even more. Everything we ask God for should be accompanied by thanksgiving.

I encourage you to examine your life, and pay attention to your thoughts, and words, and see how much thanksgiving you express. Develop an attitude of thanksgiving and watch as your relationship with God increases as He pours greater blessings than before. Thank Him today for where you are right now, and thank Him in advance for where you're about to be!!

Faith Lesson:

God knows exactly what we need when we need it and that's the exciting part of life!

Today I will...

_____

_____

_____

_____

_____

_____

_____

_____

_____

_____

_____

_____

_____

_____

_____

_____

_____

OPENLY OBEDIENT

3. Age Ain't Nothing but a Number

1 Timothy 4:12

Don't let anyone look down on you because you are young, but set an example for the believers in speech, in conduct, in love, in faith and in purity.

"Oh oh oh oh wherever I go, God is with me wherever I go," I love when Dallas sings this song at the top of his lungs! He learned the song at vacation bible school. The beautiful part about it is that I know he believes it! He knows where his strength comes from at a young age. I remember his first-grade teacher telling me how she moves him around to different groups in class. At first, I thought it was because he was being a problem child, but it turns out it was because he had a way of bringing something positive out of the other students who were surrounded by him in the classroom. I hope he never loses this trait.

OPENLY OBEDIENT

If we're honest, it's hard to follow God and be obedient to what He says, especially when you're young. You want to do what you want to do, and we live in a generation where everyone wants everything now. It's hard to stay on track and have self-control when everyone around us is doing what God told us not to do, seemingly without consequence. But we know that for every action, there is a consequence even if we don't "see" it executed. You reap what you sow, but that is also the good news.

If you sow a good seed that is what you will get back. God promises us His best. He promises us our hearts' desires. We know this, but it's tempting to take matters into our own hands. That is why teaching Dallas about Christ at a young age and being an example in the way I live is so important to me. It didn't surprise me when his teacher revealed his effect on his classmates, instead, it strengthened my faith because he reminds me so much of myself right now. That means that he is watching me. It doesn't mean that I will be perfect, but it means that now when I have the choice between what's best versus what feels better, that I will remember that I am raising up the next generation of leadership. I want him to see the effect that Jesus has on me and I want him to love the Lord himself.

Faith Lesson:

In a generation where it is easier to be a follower of your friends, choose to be a leader and follow Christ.

Today I will...

_____

_____

_____

_____

_____

_____

_____

_____

_____

_____

_____

_____

_____

_____

_____

_____

_____

_____

_____

OPENLY OBEDIENT

4. Sweet Sixteen

---

2 Corinthians 5:17

Therefore, if anyone is in Christ, he is a new creation; old things have passed away; behold, all things have become new.

Dear Sixteen-year-old Janelle,

I know that you think you're grown and know everything, but you need to listen to your mother. I know she's overprotective, but she's trying to protect you from this world. When she warns you about so-called "friends" and hanging with the wrong crowd, it's not because she doesn't want you to have a life or that she wants you to be miserable, it's because she can see what you can't. Her experience gives her an advantage. Use it for yours. Be open and listen.

She'll be the one that's there when the people you are close to now come and go. Don't try to hold on to a friendship that doesn't bring happiness into your life. You shouldn't have to be something you're not just to hang with a certain crowd. Always be your authentic self. That's what makes you who you are and that's what attracts people to you. You will gain a friend for every friend that you lose, trust me. You have your whole life ahead of you. You're going to create amazing memories. You're going to build so many strong relationships. Who you are at sixteen has nothing on who you'll be in the years to come.

You'll fall in love and it will seem so real, but in reality, you have to get to know and love yourself before you can really appreciate the meaning of true love. Yes, some people meet at sixteen and stay together forever. But you have so much to look forward to. Don't worry about love right now. Don't worry about the people who don't want you. Let them be with who they want. Trust me, you won't even think about them in a few years. You'll be free from the sweet memories and tragic "heartbreak" that you experienced with them. You're going to college in a few years and will meet so many people. People who have goals and ambition just like you. If I knew then what I know now, I would look at every relationship as a lesson learned. Learn from every heartbreak, and after every relationship, take a mental note of everything that went wrong and never go back down that road again. Don't jump to the next best thing. If someone doesn't make you happy, don't settle and stay with them. Who cares if you see them with someone else? Guess what? They'll miss you and they're going to come back around. It never fails! But you have to be strong. Never be a rebound or you'll always get treated like one. Never let a man come in and out of your life on his terms. Stand your ground, know your worth, and act accordingly.

It's okay to be single. You're singleness is your best time to learn about yourself, to know who you are, and know what you want in life. It's your time to trust and lean on God without distractions. You're so young and you're going to have all your life to be married. Wait on God. Believe in Him and pray for His will to be done in your life. Never step out and try to do things on your own. God doesn't need your help to do anything, but he does need your obedience. Be obedient to Him and life will be so much easier. No matter what happens in life, He will never leave nor forsake you. He loves you and wants the best for you. He promised to give you the desires of your heart. All you have to do is seek Him. Those are the easiest directions ever.

You're going to go far. Keep that ambition that you've always had. You've been working since you were thirteen-years-old. Learn from every single position you hold and remember the people along the way. You never know who you'll need a blessing from one day. Treat everyone with courtesy and respect. Speak to everyone and smile at them, you never know, you can be the only one that spoke to that person the entire day. A little smile can warm someone's heart and make their day. Some of the people you work with will become some of your closest friends. You meet everyone for a reason. Remember that no one can close a door that God has opened for you. You will get every job you're supposed to have. Whatever is for you will be for you.

Don't get discouraged about anything. You will get through all the tests and trials. Share your testimonies every chance you get. Your struggles will help the next person get through what you've been through. People you don't know will admire you for your transparency.

When you're able, give to others who are in need. Not to be rewarded, but because it's a blessing to be able to do that.

You will find yourself one day. You will go back to church, and thank God daily for saving you from the life you're trying to live. He will be right there with His arms open ready to receive you. You're so special to Him and He's waiting on you to return to Him. He's already in your heart. Don't keep ignoring Him. Rededicate your life to Him and watch what happens to you.

People will follow you. People will see you living a blessed life and will want to know about your God. Tell them who He is to you. Talk to God daily. Ask Him for His strength because you will need it.

Faith Lesson:

If I knew then what I know now, I would've never drifted away from God. Keep going!

Today I will...

_____

_____

_____

_____

_____

_____

_____

_____

_____

_____

_____

_____

_____

_____

_____

_____

_____

_____

_____

OPENLY OBEDIENT

5. *Disconnected*

Psalms: 34:18

**The Lord is close to the brokenhearted and saves those
who are crushed in spirit.**

I remember going to church as a young child. My best memory of church is when my mother enrolled my brothers and I in a children's church program called AWANA (Approved Workman Are Not Ashamed). This was a ministry for children to build confidence and grow in Christian faith. We would meet every Friday night, and we had weekly Bible verses to memorize. The first scripture I memorized at age nine was John 3:16. "For God so loved the world that He gave His one and only Son so that whoever believes in Him shall not perish but have eternal life." It is still my favorite scripture to this day.

Sunday mornings, my mother had us in Sunday school and over the summers we would attend Vacation Bible School. She did her absolute best to plant Jesus in our hearts and I thank her for being *that* mother.

Because I knew about Christ, I was baptized at a young age. I made the choice on my own to walk down to the altar to give my life to Christ. I took the church bus on Sunday mornings to the early morning baptism classes at my childhood church, First Baptist Church of Highland Park. I was the youngest person in the classes, but I knew at a young age I wanted Jesus in my heart. I remember after being submerged in the water, and going to dry off, my nose instantly started bleeding. I never understood why that happened, but to this day I jokingly say, "That was the blood of Jesus washing my past, present, and future sins away."

Somewhere along the way, we lost our connection. The distractions started to take over. All the enemy needed was a way in and I allowed it. I started doing things Janelle's way. I thought I was grown and no one could tell me anything. I started to be disrespectful to my mom, contemplated running away, I was just very rebellious and lost. Because I allowed the attention I received from guys to boost my confidence, I had sex for the first time at the age of thirteen. After that experience at a young age, I considered myself damaged goods. It wasn't what I told myself, but it was how I treated my body and evident in who I let touch my body.

I didn't go to church anymore. I didn't pray. I didn't do anything. I blocked God out of my life because I knew I wasn't living "right" anymore. That's exactly what the enemy wanted me to believe and I'll be the first to admit that I was his puppet and he was ruling my life.

Why would I go to church living a lifestyle I would go back to as soon as I left the church parking lot?

Just to make my mom happy, I would attend her church on Mother's Day and her birthdays. I felt the presence of God as soon as I entered the building. I knew He was pulling me to him. I knew He was missing in my life... I would feel that joyous feeling I felt when I was baptized and cry. But I would wipe my tears away before anyone would see me. I felt horrible in church because "church" wasn't on my mind. It was everything else I wanted to do when church was over that was on my mind.

When you're held in bondage to sin, what do you do? I needed the chains broken. I knew His hand was still on me and protecting me, but I was running as far away as I could. I wanted to live the way I wanted to live and didn't want to feel bad about it. I was secretly crying out, but deep down, I didn't want help.

Faith Lesson:

Your struggle will become your story to be used for His glory.

Today I will...

_____

_____

_____

_____

_____

_____

_____

_____

_____

_____

_____

_____

_____

_____

_____

_____

_____

_____

6. O. M. Gosh

Romans 8:18

For I consider that the sufferings of this present time are not worth comparing with the glory that is to be revealed to us.

I remember the day I missed my period and took a pregnancy test in the bathroom at Six Flags. Waiting on that stick to show the results took forever. My heart was beating fast, while my boyfriend at the time waited outside. When I came out the bathroom, I didn't have to say anything. I think my face said it all.

Of course, the test revealed that I was pregnant.

I was a baby, my mother's baby! And I was pregnant with a baby of my own. I was only in the 10th grade. What was I going to tell my mother? How was I going to tell my mother? Would she kick me out? Would I have to drop out of school? So many questions came to mind that I couldn't answer. So I kept my secret to myself.

For three months, no one knew I was carrying a child inside of me except my boyfriend and my cousin Shannon. She was my vault. I could tell her anything, and I knew she would be right there by my side. She was the one who took me to my first appointment.

I contemplated an abortion and even went as far as walking into Planned Parenthood to schedule the procedure, but I couldn't do it to myself. I made the decision to have sex, and this was my consequence. Plus God had other plans.

One night, I experienced the worst pain I've ever felt. I was cramping so bad to the point that I was in tears. I've had bad cramps before, but this was something indescribable. The pain wouldn't stop. I was scared, crying, and home alone.

At fifteen-years old, I experienced a miscarriage, alone on my bedroom floor.

The cramps I thought I was experiencing turned out to be contractions. I didn't take any medicine. I didn't call my mother. I cried right there until the pain went away and I fell asleep.

I wasn't mad, sad, or happy. I didn't know how I should feel. But I knew that was something I never wanted to experience again.

I needed to heal. I didn't want to have sex with a man again. And I didn't.

Faith Lesson:

At the right time, everything will make sense.

Today J will...

_____

_____

_____

_____

_____

_____

_____

_____

_____

_____

_____

_____

_____

_____

_____

_____

_____

_____

OPENLY OBEDIENT

7. *Mo*

James 1:14-15

But each person is tempted when they are dragged away by their own evil desire and enticed. Then, after desire has conceived, it gives birth to sin; and sin, when it is full-grown, gives birth to death.

I was fifteen-years-old when I walked into the gym at Calvin Coolidge Senior High School and the star basketball player caught my eye! Mo dominated that game, scoring the majority of the points and keeping the crowd cheering, including me! It felt like fate.

Later, a friend would introduce us and from that point on, we were inseparable.

At the time, I attended Largo High School and I was only at the game because my cousin was a student at Coolidge. Now, I had to figure out a way to get back. My friend and I convinced my dad to give us a ride to the game so I could see my cousin, but of course it was Mo' who I really wanted to see. As my father drove, my friend Mallory and I passed the time catching up on the latest gossip, talking about who was with who and how crazy it was that a few friends in particular had decided to "play for the other team" and date other girls.

My father was quiet, just sipping the tea we were spilling without saying a word.

We arrived during the middle of the game, and Mo was killing it again! I ended up sitting on the opposing team's side, so I had to walk on the court to get to the home side. As I crossed the court, I know I caught Mo's eye. I still remember the gray velour sweat suit I had on, looking good if I do say so myself. Mo was the leading scorer that night, and it was because of my presence, I'm sure... Somewhere between the car ride and picking me up from the game, my father did some snooping on my Black Planet page.

When we got back in the car after the game, Mallory and I were still talking about the latest news, but little did I know that he was listening intently and that I was only digging myself into a deeper hole. I was confirming things that he suspected from my social media page. Somehow from looking at the pictures on my page, he had pieced together that the "Mo" I was referencing was short for Monique.

When he dropped me off at my mom's house he let me have it. My father was in tears. REAL TEARS. He couldn't even get his words out. He was so hurt and I saw it all in his face. I didn't know something like that would hurt him. He put me on punishment, canceled my sixteenth birthday party, and took my phone away from me. Of course I was angry about my party and phone, but honestly, I was more upset that he (the man that wasn't around) put me on "punishment." He didn't even live there to put me on punishment in that house. I was livid! One thing I never did was have the courage to "talk back" to my father, so all of my anger was of course, in my mind. I never admitted anything to him. It was my secret and I was sticking to it. My mother was oblivious to the reason behind my punishment. I don't remember him telling her anything about Mo' and I know I never did.

Monique made me feel comfortable. She was the first female I brought around my friends. She was the first for many things. I remember the day she came up to my high school just to show me that she had my name tattooed on the back of her shoulder. Listen, we were serious! But I never brought anyone home and introduced them as my girlfriend. I just couldn't. I thought it would be a phase, but the deeper things became, the more discomfort I felt in my spirit. It felt like a game of tug-of-war. I wanted to get out of this lifestyle, but my flesh wanted every ounce of it.

Something needed to change, so I just started to pray. I started asking God to remove the desires of other women from my mind. I couldn't handle being disconnected from God any longer. I prayed daily, "Lead me not to temptation, but deliver me."

I slowly started to focus back on God. I didn't lose my desire overnight, it took me years to break free from the lifestyle. No matter what has disconnected you from God, remember He's waiting on your return. He never leaves you nor forsakes you. He's right there all the time with His arms open wide waiting. He will forgive you no matter what you do.

Faith Lesson:

God helped David defeat Goliath against all odds, so whatever needs to be defeated in my life, God can do that too!

Today I will...

_____

_____

_____

_____

_____

_____

_____

_____

_____

_____

_____

_____

_____

_____

_____

_____

_____

8. Love Ain't Marriage

Psalm 30:5

For His anger *is but for* a moment, His favor *is for* life; Weeping may endure for a night, but joy *comes* in the morning.

I had a boyfriend that I thought I could be with forever. He was my best friend. I shared so much of myself with him, so much of my life, my dreams, my family, everything. I made him my husband in my mind.

This was my first real relationship with a guy, and I put a lot of pressure on him. We met in 2005 at North Carolina A&T (Aggie Pride!) and started fooling around with each other in 2008. As friends, we used to have some amazing conversations. He was a "ladies man" and the first man I fooled around with in over six years. He was such a gentleman and made me wonder why I ever left guys alone. I remember our first Christmas together. He came over to my mom's house with a huge wrapped gift box. Inside of the huge box were at least five other little boxes. I kept opening one box just to find another empty box. The last box had a letter in it that read "kiss me for your gift." It was so cute. It reminded me of something my father would do if he had a surprise for me. When they were all opened, he had gotten me a Tiffany's necklace, a new iPod and a cute little wallet. I cried like a baby. He always bought me gifts and took me to the best restaurants. He jokingly tells me how he "started me" on my lifestyle. He definitely did introduce me to *real.* The gifts and the money didn't make him a nice guy, he just treated me with respect and honored me. He loved and respected his mother, and you know what they say; if he treats his mother well, he will treat you well too. He was just an all-around great guy.

I graduated before him so he was still in North Carolina for a while. We both liked going to the clubs, and just being out all the time. We were young! I had my friends and he had his friends but because we went to college together, most of our friends were all the same. Life was fun together. No cares, no huge responsibilities, just us.

And then I got pregnant with Dallas.

Even during my pregnancy, we still had fun together. Of course we weren't doing what we used to do to have fun, but we made our own fun and created memories with each other and my growing belly.

It wasn't until Dallas was born that I became "boring." He never called me boring, but I felt like I was boring. All I could do was work and be a mommy. I wasn't making him a priority anymore. And when you know you're not doing your job, it makes you think someone else is doing your job. At least that's how I thought.

I started to doubt his love for me. When I was in the house with our child, he was still out doing the things we used to do together. He was in the club while I was changing diapers and he was going out when I was going to bed. Soon I became suspicious.

I couldn't put my finger on it, but I knew something wasn't right. My women's intuition was getting the best of me. I could feel that he was up to something, but when I would ask him questions, it would turn into arguments or I just seemed crazy, since I didn't have evidence.

We went downhill fast.

I was in a relationship with a guy I didn't trust, but I couldn't leave him alone. I was determined to find out what he was up to... I wanted to catch him, so I went looking! They say if you seek you will find. That's exactly what happened. I found out he cheated on me.

My investigative side hacked into his email account and that's when I realized that woman's intuition is real. It was right there in my face, I read everything: how it was initiated, how it ended, and how it was about to happen again. I read it over and over again. It was like turning the knife in an already open wound.

I called him and confronted him about it. He denied it and hung up on me. My trust in him died that day. He let me feel crazy just to cover up his dirt.

It wasn't until I sent him screenshots of the email thread that he admitted it. That hurt. I had to have evidence to get the truth. What happened to communication and honesty?

Why lie to me? Why keep me around? If I wasn't making him happy, why not just break up with me? I'm sure I called him every name in the book and meant every word of it. How could he cheat on me? I did everything I could to make sure our relationship was good.

I cried on the inside at work. I went home that day and cried some more. I cried for at least a week straight. That night, I didn't get any sleep. I replayed the words in the email in my head. Every time I dozed off, I jumped up as if I was waking up from a nightmare. I was sweating and my heart was racing. I really wanted it all to be a dream. My nights went on like that for months.

I prayed for peace. I couldn't keep going like this. I was headed towards depression.

Things got better between us, and then I went back!

I knew he was a great man, and he had my back like no other. I could call on him for anything. However, I still did not trust him. I trusted him with my life, but not my heart. I knew he wouldn't let anything happen to me, but I wouldn't allow him to have my heart ever again. I loved him, yes, but the selfish me didn't want to see him with anyone else. I would think about all the memories we had and didn't want another woman to experience that. This time around, he constantly tried to prove his loyalty to me, but I still did not trust him. I reminded him all the time. It wasn't fair to either of us. We were both settling for each other. Nothing could come out of this relationship except the love we had for our child.

It was time to let go. While neither one of us were perfect, I'm thankful that we were wise enough to go our separate ways without another tragic fall out. That's one of the best decisions we could've ever made. We were young and have learned from our mistakes. He is still a great guy, he still respects me and we do an amazing job co-parenting, and that's all I can ask from him. As long as our child is good, we're good. We say that all the time.

This relationship has taught me to never be with someone because we're comfortable. If you can't trust someone, evaluate why. If it's something you think you can never get through, don't stay in the relationship.

I pressured him to be the man I wanted him to be. Yes, he was my boyfriend. Yes, he was the father of my son. But he was never my husband. Sex bonded us together, not God.

Faith Lesson:

God will make a comfortable situation uncomfortable to lead you to where you need to be.

Today I will...

_____

_____

_____

_____

_____

_____

_____

_____

_____

_____

_____

_____

_____

_____

_____

_____

_____

_____

_____

9. My Missing Puzzle Piece

Psalm 139:13 14

For you created my inmost being; you knit me together in my mother's womb. I praise you because I am Fearfully and Wonderfully made; your works are wonderful. I know that full well.

September 28, 2010 was one of the best days of my life! Nineteen hours of labor and a C-section later, I heard Dallas' first cry. I remember it like it was yesterday, looking at the ceiling in Southern Maryland Hospital, holding his father's hand, praying quietly to God for a healthy baby boy. A white sheet separated me from seeing what the doctors were doing. I wished that something could have eliminated the pressure of them cutting me open and pulling Dallas out. Moments later out came Dallas. When I heard his first cry, all I could do was thank God. I cried aloud, "That's my baby. My baby is here." I didn't see him in that moment. All I heard was the doctor's voice, "Boy he has a big head." I didn't see Dallas until I came out of recovery a few hours later, and I couldn't stop staring at him and all that hair. He was seven pounds and six ounces of perfect. And he was mine. "But what now? What do I do now," I thought. I didn't know the first thing about being a mother. What was I supposed to do? And just like that, at twenty-three years old, I was ushered into motherhood. It was now my responsibility to love him, to feed him, to nourish him, and to protect him.

I wanted a bond with him that nobody else could have. But that didn't go as planned. After reading all of the mommy books and blogs while pregnant, I wanted to experience that instant bond that all the blogs talked about, but I didn't. When it came time to feed him, Dallas didn't latch on to me and I thought something was wrong with me. The bond that I had heard about just wasn't there no matter how hard I tried. I wanted to love Dallas the way he should have been loved, but I couldn't. Trust me I tried. If I wasn't living with my mother at the time, I don't know where I would be. It's like I wanted him in the house with me, but I didn't want to be right next to him. I was able to give him to my mom and lock myself in the room. I couldn't even give him his first bath, because I was still recovering from my C-section. I was suffering from Postpartum Depression. I'm thankful that my mom eventually encouraged me to talk to a doctor and get some help. Once I found out that the way I felt was common, things began to smooth out. Again, this was not an overnight process, but in time things changed for the better. The love I have for Dallas today is unconditional and unexplainable.

He's literally my best friend. We have amazing talks about life, God, family plans, and more. I can't imagine my life without him. He motivates me like no other. I see so much of my personality in him. He is a real comedian just like his mommy. He's a lover, a giver, and a protector... Every morning, we lock our pinkies together and say, "I love you and I'm so glad Jesus put us together." And it's so true. God makes no mistakes. He has blessed me with this little boy for a reason and I'm just soaking up all the love.

Faith Lesson:

Treat your children like gifts from God Himself,
because that's exactly what they are.

Today I will...

_____

_____

_____

_____

_____

_____

_____

_____

_____

_____

_____

_____

_____

_____

_____

_____

_____

10. The Breakthrough

Psalm 34:17-19

The righteous cry out and the Lord hears them; he delivers them from all their troubles. The Lord is close to the brokenhearted and saves those who are crushed in spirit. The righteous person may have many troubles, but the Lord delivers him from them all.

One Saturday morning, I was cleaning my old apartment when I broke down in the middle of my living room and just cried out to God. I needed Him so badly. I couldn't make it on my own anymore. I couldn't think negative about life anymore. I needed Him to come fill those voids that were in my heart and remove the anger I had buried deep down inside. I had nowhere to turn. I had to stop running to other people for peace.

That cry for God awakened something inside of me. It removed the pain and thoughts that eventually would have taken my life. The next morning I went to church! I had heard so much about the First Baptist Church of Glenarden that I made a decision to visit that Sunday morning. I can't remember the message, but I know it had me in tears the entire time.

God used Pastor John K. Jenkins to speak to me, at least that's how I felt. I went that Sunday and then three consecutive Sundays after that.

On the forth Sunday I boldly walked down to the altar with Dallas on my hip and rededicated my life to Christ, joined the church, and started my personal walk with Christ. Prior to this moment, the enemy had a hold on me. That devil had me at a very low place in my life. It was a place where alcohol couldn't cure me. Sex couldn't cure me. Gifts couldn't cure me. Nothing could cure me but being back in His arms. I've never been happier or had so much peace in my life. Being back in God's arms after doing things your way for years will make you apologetic. You know you don't deserve what He gives you but that's how good He is! He doesn't give us what we deserve. God pulled me out of my mess in time to save me before I drifted too far away from Him. He was there with open arms to forgive me when I repented of my sins and apologized for straying away. My slate was clean.

I know I'm right where God wants me to be.

This didn't happen overnight. I was very hard headed. I am one of those people who has to learn things the hard way. Despite all that I've been through, it took a heartbreak to get my attention. I couldn't have written my own story that way, but I thank Him for it.

Learning is a process—one that honestly never ends. We are all unique and each have our own journey, but the beauty of it all is that along our way, He is always there.

THE BREAKTHROUGH

If you grew up in a Christian household, then I'm sure you've seen the poem "Footprints." It's a conversation between "man" and God that illustrates this truth.

Man says to God, "Lord you said once I decided to follow you, you'd walk with me all the way. But I noticed during the saddest most troubling parts of my life, there was only one set of footprints. I don't understand why, when I needed you the most, you would leave me."

God whispered, "My precious child, I love you and will never leave you. Never, ever, during your trials and testing. When you only saw one set of footprints, it was then that I carried you."

Many people question why God allows us to go through all of our stuff before we can experience a breakthrough, but the truth is even when you feel alone, and hopeless, and are wondering why God isn't there, He is. Sometimes all you have to do is cry out!

Faith Lesson:

The closer you get to God, the closer you will get to your breakthrough.

Today I will...

_____

_____

_____

_____

_____

_____

_____

_____

_____

_____

_____

_____

_____

_____

_____

_____

_____

11. A Change is Gonna Come

Ecclesiastes 3:1

For everything there is a season, and a time for every matter under heaven.

If you're following my timeline, you may have noticed that I was having sex since I was thirteen-years-old. I had a miscarriage when I was fifteen, and before I had time to heal, I met Monique a few months later. Things didn't work out with her and for the next six years, I was in and out of relationships with other women. After that lifestyle, I still didn't give my heart and body time to heal or rest. I then got involved with Dallas' dad. Clearly, I was all over the place! I needed to take time for Janelle. But of course, I didn't stop there. I was looking for love in all the wrong places.

I met "Mr. Big" during the time I *thought* I was healing from a broken heart. He was the definition of a real man. Not because he was almost twice my age, but because he had his priorities together. He was very successful, mentally and physically strong, and a provider. He knew who he was, what he wanted, and he was grateful for what he had. He helped to transform me into a woman. I started to carry myself differently. I started to dress differently, and I looked at life differently. Life with Mr. Big gave me a new worldview. He was very wise, and I loved how he brought something out of me that guys my age weren't talking about. He was the one to talk to me about managing my money, saving, and credit. Because of him, I opened up my first credit card and he helped me pay it on time every month. He introduced me to the materialistic lifestyle...Life was good.

But deep down I still wasn't healed. And it showed in my actions and attitude towards him. He was a great guy, but of course I sabotaged our relationship.

I don't know what I was searching for, but I started to love the attention I was getting. I was a real woman! And real men wanted real women, right?

I became an attention seeker and lived for attention. There was a time when I would give my number to anybody just to see what they were about.

I hated talking on the phone, but I would text a guy all day and all night. Texting turned into going on dates, and I never turned down a free meal. I became a serial dater, but in hindsight, I was selling myself short. I wasted my time being in the presence of people I saw no future with.

This lifestyle and mindset lasted for a few years until enough was enough.

One day after work I walked into my regular hangout spot. After talking to a guy at the bar for a while, he paid for my tab. Then, he asked for my number. I wasn't attracted to him, the conversation was weak, and there was no connection whatsoever. I didn't want to give him my number, but I did it anyway.

I could block him later.

That was my cycle when I felt lonely.

But that day something shifted. I knew it would be the last time.

No sooner than I got in my car, he texted me. I blocked him. That's when I knew it was time for a change.

Faith Lesson:

You always know when it's time to let go...
trust your gut!

Today J will...

_____

_____

_____

_____

_____

_____

_____

_____

_____

_____

_____

_____

_____

_____

_____

_____

_____

_____

12. Not so F.A.S.T

Joel 1:14

Consecrate a fast, call a sacred assembly; gather the elders and all the inhabitants of the land into the house of the LORD your God, and cry out to the LORD.

Fasting is purposefully and voluntarily abstaining from a pleasurable activity. It is a discipline to focus our attention from our flesh and toward God. Anything that can be given up temporarily in order to focus on and grow closer to God can be considered a fast. One of the keys to a successful fast is staying in close communication with God. Fasting and prayer goes hand-in-hand. Would you want to miss something God has for you only because you didn't fast and pray?

It isn't an easy thing to do and the irony is that the process is slow. It can take a while to build up to a full fast and can be quite uncomfortable, but that is the point. Take those hunger pangs and turn them in prayers.

I remember my first time fasting. It was in January of 2013 while I was in the Queen Esther Ministry at the First Baptist Church of Glenarden. I had heard so many great testimonies about fasting, how God answered specific prayers, and how people received revelation about themselves, so I was excited to experience it all. It was a month-long fast to abstain from meats, sweets, and television. Sounds easy right? Wrong! It was hard. To go a month without my strawberry fruit snacks, crispy bacon, and TV? That was tough! There were plenty of times when I wanted to give in and satisfy my flesh, but I remember how much I wanted to experience this deeper relationship with Christ. I wanted to hear from Him. I wanted Him to answer my prayers, and I wanted to prove to myself how much self-control and obedience I had.

During the fast, the enemy was trying to deter me from finishing strong. At times, I asked myself, "Am I doing this right?"

"Shouldn't something be happening?"

"I'm not hearing from God" and "why should I finish this?" This was my first fast and I didn't know what to expect, so I was just trying to go with the flow. I definitely had my weak moments, but prayer really helped me through, along with the encouragement of other ladies in the ministry. See, I couldn't talk to everybody about it since fasting is something we do discreetly. When you fast, it should be between you and God. But because we fasted as a ministry, we had other women to hold us accountable.

At first, I didn't have anything specific to pray for, but a few days in, I started telling myself, "I'm fasting for favor." I wanted God to have favor on me, to open up doors that only He can open.

Before the fast, I was praying about a specific job that I really wanted and had been denied previously. During the fast, I prayed for a turnaround. I prayed specifically for God to show Himself mighty and strong and to do the unthinkable.

Within that month of January, I received a letter stating that I was eligible to appeal the denial for the job. Right there at that moment, I experienced favor from God. No, this letter didn't say I had the job, but I knew the letter itself was nothing but God. It was a way for God to tell me, "I see you; I hear you; now stay patient and hold on." I can't even explain the feeling I experienced, but it was definitely an encounter with God. That wasn't the only way I experienced God. Since I wasn't watching television, my goal was to be out of the house as much as possible. An idle mind is the devil's playground, and I didn't want him to have any room in my mind to taunt or tempt me.

When you're fasting, you gain clear direction and hear from God about what He needs you to do and where you need to be. One Saturday morning, I felt the urge to go over to my grandmother's house. When I arrived, I walked into the middle of a conversation regarding this new great home buying program in Washington, DC. My aunt began telling me about a program her daughter was in to get her home, and some benefits for DC residents. At the time I was renting my apartment in Southeast and I knew I didn't want to be there forever. I knew that walking in to this conversation was of course orchestrated by God. I didn't know at the time, but I know now that this desire of mine was God's next plan for my life. He wanted me to become a homeowner. He was making provisions for me to get to my next step. My aunt didn't know, but she was planting a seed that would get me on track.

I was denied the job for financial issues. So just think, during this fast, I received a letter to appeal a decision that denied me a job because of my finances, and I knew my next step was to get involved in the home-buying process. This was God setting me up for a double blessing, and I didn't even know it. Not only did I have to get my finances together for the job, but I needed to get my finances together to buy a home. You see how all things work together for our good? I'm not done yet. My lease was up in January too, so I knew another way for me to stay on top of my finances was to save as much money as I could. I prayed long and hard about it and God told me to go back home with my mother. Sacrificing my space and being obedient to God paid off.

I stayed at my mom's house for eighteen months. During this time, I was able to save the mortgage amount that I was comfortable with for my future home. For example, if I wanted my mortgage to be $1,600, that's the amount I would save every month to make sure I was financially stable with what I had left over. The money I saved in that year paid for my down payment and closing costs for my house. Being a homeowner today is a result of my first fast in 2013. I closed on my house in August 2014, and two weeks later, I started my new job. Thee job!

I've fasted so many times after my first fast. To this day, I fast whenever I need to free myself from things and people. I fast from social media more than anything, but I also fast from fast food, shopping, being on my phone after a certain time, and much more. I do this to allow God to have His time with me. Instead of being on social media, I could read a book, write a book, play games with my son, anything. Fasting is a time to deny your flesh and to nurture your spirit.

There are so many things that God wants to tell us and reveal to us, but we must be willing to sit and listen to Him.

While fasting, the enemy will try to attack you because he knows how powerful a fast can be and the benefits you can receive. Your eyes will be open to what God has for you. You will hear His voice, prayers will be answered, strongholds will be broken, and so much more. I encourage everyone to fast and when you do, keep pressing. The enemy is going to try everything to break that closeness that you're trying to experience with God. You can't give up, you have to finish strong. And you will.

Faith Lesson

Fast.

F-Focus on God.

A-Abstain from whatever God is telling you.

S-Surrender to God.

T-Trust in Him to see you through.

Today I will...

_____

_____

_____

_____

_____

_____

_____

_____

_____

_____

_____

_____

_____

_____

_____

_____

_____

_____

_____

13. *Breaking the Cycle*

Matthew 6:33

**But seek first the kingdom of God and His righteous-
ness, and all these things shall be added to you.**

On August 9, 2016, I made the decision to break the cycles
in my life. A friend whom I will call "siAmese" gave me the
confirmation I needed to start my fast. She was almost fin-
ished with the same fast when I told her how God told me to
stop giving my number out. I wanted to be obedient to God,
and I changed my number. I vowed to go an entire year—yes
365 days of no men. No texting, no dates, and of course, no
sex.

That day at my kitchen table, after getting off the phone
with Sprint, I felt relieved, lost, and excited at the same time.
Relieved because I was now free from people having instant
access to me. Relieved because I now had a clean slate.

Relieved because I was going all in for Christ and letting Him have His way with me. But lost, because this was so new to me. I've had the same number for years, so just imagine the contacts and connections I lost.

I knew for the next 365 days I wouldn't have a man to entertain me. This was very new for me. I've always had someone to text and to give me attention. I even removed my male best friend and close girlfriends' contact information from my phone. When I changed my number, I didn't tell everyone nor did I give an explanation. Honestly, I didn't think I was strong enough to make it the entire time and I wasn't going to let anyone know I failed.

It wasn't easy to stay on track, but I made a vow and there was no turning around now. When I felt weak, my circle of friends would cheer me on and remind me of why I started. They understood that I needed a break and they were happy to witness my journey. They knew I was running in circles and getting nowhere. But what happened next was mind blowing.

God had me alone. All to himself. He used that time to intentionally prepare me to be the person I am today. I gained strength to keep pressing. Strength that only God could give me. I found peace with myself and started to recognize why I kept repeating those cycles. It was peace that passes all understanding. I spoke life into myself on a daily basis. I didn't have to waste any more time looking for love in all the wrong places. I started to truly believe that I was worthy of love because I discovered self-love. I learned not to lean on my own understanding by trusting the process. I found out what it means to let God have total control of me. I asked Him to guide and direct my steps every day. I even started cooking.

God is so intentional. He placed me around Godly women who empowered me to step out of my box. Divine opportunities were orchestrated all around me. More importantly, I learned that I couldn't run to anybody else for healing because true peace and healing comes from Jesus.

I learned that alone didn't mean lonely. Instead, sometimes God needs you by yourself to make you whole and to prepare you for your next blessing. He needed to work out some habits and insecurities that I had that could potentially keep me from reaching my next level. It wasn't an easy year, but it was some of the best moments of my life.

If I didn't take the time to intentionally break the cycles in my life, I don't know where I would be. I was on the road to becoming the total opposite of the woman God was transforming me into.

Faith Lesson:

Today make a vow, and decide that there is no turning around now and watch God wow!

Today I will...

_____

_____

_____

_____

_____

_____

_____

_____

_____

_____

_____

_____

_____

_____

_____

_____

_____

14. Daddy Pains

Matthew 7:9-11

Which of you, if your son asks for bread, will give him a stone? Or if he asks for fish, will give him a snake? If you, then, though you are evil, know how to give good gifts to your children, how much more will your father in heaven give good gifts to those who ask Him.

One Sunday night, my dad stopped by to fix my television. I made some amazing ribs the night before, so I offered him some. He tore those ribs up! That was my first time making ribs, so seeing him demolish the ribs made me so proud! As he cleaned the bone, he jokingly said, "If you cook like this, I'll have to come over here every Sunday." Although I knew it was just another way of complimenting my cooking, a lightbulb went off in my head. What if we continued to do this every Sunday?

"You're more than welcome to come over next week," I replied. I saw it as a chance for us to spend some much-needed time together. This relationship was so important to me, because I needed to know my father loved me, and I needed to know him to truly love him.

For many years, I was walking around with "Daddy Pains," searching for the love I needed from my father in the guys I dated. Growing up, I always thought the "good ol' boys" were too good to be true. Therefore, I was attracted to the "bad boys." I wanted to be with the guys who I had to make love me. I was attracted to the guys who were known to be with all the ladies. I saw it as a challenge to make them choose me. And they did. They chose me along with every other girl who was attracted to them. I was addicted to the pain though. I thought that's what love was. I didn't know how love from a man should feel, but unconsciously, it looked unavailable and hard to get. When good guys came around who wanted to stick around, I somehow found a way to sabotage those relationships, because I figured it wouldn't last long. But there was a time when receiving gifts made me stick around. I wasn't convinced that they loved me if they couldn't show me something in my hand. My father was known for buying me things. He would come around on Christmas with the best Christmas gifts. My birthday is three days before Valentine's Day, so he would come around with a ton of balloons and chocolate too. This set the tone for the way I expected other people to show their love for me. I still remember my fourth grade boyfriend Vincent, who stole his mother's expensive perfume to give to me! I received an expensive North Face coat in the tenth grade, and for my sixteenth birthday, I remember the principal at Largo High School calling me into his office to have my mother come pick-up all the balloons that I had received in school. That materialistic mindset of mine went on well into my adulthood, especially when I met "Mr. Big!" You clearly needed a good J-O-B to be with me.

I talked to my dad about this and more one night at the dinner table. He told me that he didn't know how to love because it wasn't shown to him. He didn't know how to open up, because nobody opened up to him. My mom and dad have been married for over thirty years, but only lived together for maybe four of those years. I was finally able to understand where my ideas of love came from. I also realized that I wanted love in my life to be different. I wanted a love defined more by moments like the ones we had over dinner than how many dollars someone spent on me.

I didn't care if it took thirty years for this to happen, because having this new relationship with my dad has brought me healing and closer to God! I knew I couldn't fully love a man if I didn't love my own father. It just makes me feel so good knowing I have this man in my corner rooting for me and telling me how amazing I am. But it's more special to me because he's not just any man, but he's my DADDY! I know he loves me, not because of what he buys me, but because he tells me and shows me his love.

Faith Lesson:

Make a consistent effort to communicate with the Father in your home and the one on the throne. If either relationship is broken, do your best to fix it.

Today I will...

_____

_____

_____

_____

_____

_____

_____

_____

_____

_____

_____

_____

_____

_____

_____

_____

15. Faith on Fleek

Hebrews 11:6

And without faith it is impossible to please God, because anyone who comes to him must believe that he exists and that he rewards those who earnestly seek him.

"Faith on Fleek" is a saying I've been using for a couple of years. It means that my faith in God is undeniable. Faith is the ability to trust God. It is having the confidence that He will work everything out. I have enough faith to believe that God will do exceedingly and abundantly more than I can imagine. He has shown on many occasions, that if I surrender to him, He will handle the rest. I am confident in asking Him for anything, and I believe He will favor me to give me what I ask for if I'm supposed to have it. I've seen Him do the impossible in my life. He has done things that only He can do. I've seen miracles happen because of my faith.

If He told you that you can have the desires of your heart, but it will take five years before He gives it to you, would you wait on him?

If He would have told me that it would take two years for me to clean up my credit and start my new job, I would have given up. Or if He told me years ago that I would be single for six years and counting, I probably would have settled instead of being alone. But He makes us go through things that don't make sense at first knowing that we will understand in time.

As much as I dislike "the wait," I love the process. When I'm waiting on God, I'm praying specifically for my desires. I enjoy expecting what I'm praying for, and I enjoy not knowing how it'll come to me. Most of all, I enjoy knowing whatever God gives me will surpass the requests I made to Him. While we wait, He is putting all the puzzle pieces together so it will be perfect for us when it's our time.

I can't say the waiting period isn't hard, because it is. But during the process, we have to stay connected, continue to obey, and remember to praise Him. Spend time getting to know Him and understand why you're waiting.

Faith Lesson:

Faith is a requirement for a walk with God.

Today I will...

_____

_____

_____

_____

_____

_____

_____

_____

_____

_____

_____

_____

_____

_____

_____

_____

_____

_____

OPENLY OBEDIENT

16. Good Girl Gone God

1 Corinthians 10:13

No temptation has overtaken you except such as is common to man; but God *is* faithful, who will not allow you to be tempted beyond what you are able, but with the temptation will also make the way of escape, that you may be able to bear *it.*

I do not want to give the impression that rededicating my life to Christ automatically solved all my problems. I still have struggles. You've heard the saying, "It's so hard to be good and so easy to be bad." I feel like that every time I let my flesh win and I do the things I want to do but shouldn't do; things I know I will regret right after I do them. It's easy to live in the moment and give in to temptation. Think about all the times God took you out of bad situations and you promised yourself you'd never go back. But then you went back.

Or is that only me? Am I the only one that will admit that I allow my flesh to win at times?

I'm telling you that as a Godly woman who wants to make good decisions, that it isn't always easy. There is a battle taking place and what you're struggling with is your desire to elevate—to elevate above what your flesh and body want versus what your soul and spirit need to level up.

It's what happens when you are trying to go from good to God. Don't believe for one second that if you're still struggling, you're a bad person.

Giving in to temptation can make you feel like that though, but it's all a part of the devil's plan. If he can make you feel bad, you start to trust yourself less and less. Soon you will rationalize that since you have no self-control that this must be who you are, and so you will stop being intentional about your walk with God. That is where the enemy wants you!

When I give in to temptation, I get so upset with myself because I have to start all the way over again. I have to start my countdown all over again. I have to begin at day one of no *this* (fill in the blank) or day one of no *that.* I guess that's why Lamentations 3:22–24 reminds us that, in Christ, the Lord will be faithful to be there every morning with enough new mercy to get us through today's troubles, sin, and pain.

Temptation is real, and, it's everywhere. The enemy knows our weak spots and he will repeatedly employ every tool in his toolbox to get us where he wants us. For me, the enemy knows I made the decision to practice celibacy. I've chosen to purposefully save myself for my husband on our wedding night to experience "us" together for the first time as husband and wife. I have decided and committed to God that I want what he gives me more than anything. I want my God-given peace, clarity, and power more than I want to have sex. Don't get me wrong; sex is great, but it clouds my judgement. You know the feeling when you stay with a person although you know deep down inside that you're not happy? You say it's love, but in reality, it's a soul tie. That's honestly the worst place to be—stuck in bondage because of sex, and you can't leave. I've been there many times… when I knew the person didn't treat me right, knew I deserved better, knew I could actually do better, but I stayed. I don't want to create a soul tie with anyone else. A soul tie is a linkage in the soul realm between two people. It links the two souls together, which can be a good or a bad thing. Yes, a soul tie isn't always a bad thing. It's only bad when it's with the wrong person. I want my soul tie ordained by God and only with the soul mate He has for me. I've given my sexuality to Him and I trust that He will tell me the person worthy enough for me. I know that I have to be free from bondage to go where God is leading me.

I wouldn't lie to anyone and say this is easy, because it's definitely not. The enemy knows about my decision to be celibate and how obedient I want to be. Imagine how hard he's making it for me. As you can see, I'm not a virgin, so I know firsthand how IT feels. So, celibacy is definitely a struggle. Not only do I struggle with the feeling of wanting sex, but I also struggle with my thoughts and desires. I have to renew my mind daily, and a big part of that is being mindful of what I watch and hear. I've learned that what we watch and listen to shows up in our lifestyles. Whatever you allow to occupy your mind will soon determine your speech and actions. I can't speak for everyone, but that's what I've learned.

This is an everyday battle. There are plenty of times when I want to have a late night rendezvous (and I've tried), but I know how I would feel afterwards. It would set me back, and it would quench my flesh for just that moment. It's hard because I know God promised me His best, but I honestly get tired of waiting. But when I settle for right now, it always turns out to be the wrong option.

For these reasons, I'm choosing celibacy. Let me be clear on what that means since we live in a society with so much grey area. I made the decision to abstain from sex! I want to prove to myself and God that I can deny myself instant gratification. I did this during my One Year Man Fast. I proved to myself that I really can do all things through Christ. As bad as I want to have sex, I get an even bigger thrill when I deny my flesh. I call it sexual integrity.

Oh God, now it's all out there. I hesitated to write this because Lord forbid I slip up after sharing this decision. I'm doing it anyway though, because I know that I am not alone. I also know that we don't share this part of our journeys enough, and by doing so, it will make me hold myself more accountable—not because I have something to prove, but because I'm confessing my decision and I want to be free from my past soul ties to be ready for my husband. I've realized over time how God always provides a way of escape when we're tempted, so I'm trusting Him to get me through this, one day at a time! Just like everything else in life, as long as we're living, every day is just day one anyway. Stay strong today!

Faith Lesson:

God always provides a way of escape. Look out for it the next time you're tempted, and choose to walk away. Put boundaries in place and know your limits.

Today I will...

_____

_____

_____

_____

_____

_____

_____

_____

_____

_____

_____

_____

_____

_____

_____

_____

_____

_____

OPENLY OBEDIENT

17. Things Aren't Always What They Seem

Proverbs 4:23

Above all else, guard your heart, for everything you do flows from it.

There was a time when I used to wake up and get on social media before anything else. I have a love/hate relationship with social media. I love that it's my platform to witness to others, to keep in touch with family members, and I believe it's an amazing marketing tool for business owners, but I hate what it does to people, including me.

You know that saying, "A picture says a thousand words?" I believe it. I'll be the first to tell you that I am not perfect. Neither is my life. I love to share what God is up to in my life, but I don't share my struggles. No one does. I've learned that the same person you're admiring from afar has their own issues that they are working on just like you. No one is perfect, no matter how perfect their pictures look.

I have to discipline myself when it comes to social media. I've had to make a conscious effort to limit my time on Facebook, Instagram, Twitter, and Snapchat. It can send me down a rabbit hole pretty quickly. Sometimes, I can spend hours looking at the lives of complete strangers and comparing my life to theirs because their pictures portray their best lives. I have totally disregarded all the blessings God has already given me. I owe it to myself to take breaks to renew my mind and to get me back on track. Time off of social media helps me to remember that I too have it going on. At times, social media made me feel like I wasn't good enough or that I needed more in life.

When I get on social media now, I post about God's work in my life. I love it because it's my platform to speak about Jesus Christ. I know when I share a testimony on Facebook, my inbox is flooded with believers and also those who want to know Christ more. It's a way for my "friends" to see what God has done in my life. It's an opportunity for others to see how God is using me so they can see that God can use them too. I realize that social media may not be everyone's issue, but we all have something. Whatever your issue, put boundaries in place to guard your heart from the tricks of the enemy and practice self-control because things aren't always what they seem.

Faith Lesson:

Don't compare your entire life to someone's highlight reel.

Today I will...

_____

_____

_____

_____

_____

_____

_____

_____

_____

_____

_____

_____

_____

_____

_____

_____

_____

OPENLY OBEDIENT

18. Single and Saved

1 Corinthians 7:34

An unmarried woman or virgin is concerned about the Lord's affairs: Her aim is to be devoted to the Lord in both body and spirit. But a married woman is concerned about the affairs of this world—how she can please her husband.

It's hard being single.

It's harder being single *and* saved. I didn't take a year away from men to go right back down the same path of going on pointless dates and giving my number to anyone. Been there, done that.

Being single and saved means being selective and waiting on God to bring the person He has for you. Now let's be clear, you're not literally sitting around waiting doing nothing. You are living your best life. You should be getting to know your self inside and out. You should know your interests, your wants, your dislikes. More importantly, you should cherish this time to get closer to God. Create a bond so strong that you know his likeness when you see it.

Although the movies want you to believe that you are looking for someone to complete you, each person should already come to the relationship complete. When you do that, you'll find someone who compliments you and you won't just jump at any opportunity because it's convenient or because you're bored.

I really believe that's how God works. Imagine this:

You're going to the gym three days a week because you are focused on working on your health and fitness. Over the past few weeks, you've noticed Mr. Tall and Handsome, who you occasionally say hello to, but nothing more, because again, you're there to focus on yourself. Then, on Sunday at church, when they ask if there are any first-time visitors, a familiar face sitting in the row in front of you raises his hand. It's him—Mr. Tall and Handsome from the gym! After a conversation in the lobby, you learn he has noticed you, but he too was focused on his health and fitness. He knew that he needed more and decided to go to church that day, and he officially met you. After an amazing talk, he tells you that he hopes to see you at the gym on Monday and you part ways.

Maybe this is the start of something.

Maybe it's not, but if it is, it didn't start from a place of desperation. You didn't have to go bar hopping hoping to meet someone when that's not even your thing. It would be sparked from mutual interests, a mutual way of looking at life. Not rushed, or even rooted in romance, just friendship and a love for fitness.

I don't know about you, but I want different results in life and I can't keep doing the same thing expecting different results. I want to be married, and I want my marriage to symbolize Christ's love for the church. I want to be in love and have that companionship with one man until death do us part.

I want this man to love me like no other. I want to show the generations to come that marriage does work.

I know what I want in a man. I know that I deserve a good Christian man. And I know because I'm fully submitted to Christ, He will give me His best. His desires became my desires. And this is why I will wait on Him to bring who He has for me. I will continue praying for discernment and trusting His way because the enemy comes in all shapes, sizes, and designer cologne scents, and I don't want to be distracted again.

Faith Lesson:

Dating with a purpose makes you confident enough to walk away from someone who doesn't value your worth. But first, you have to know your worth.

Today I will...

_____

_____

_____

_____

_____

_____

_____

_____

_____

_____

_____

_____

_____

_____

_____

_____

_____

_____

_____

19. Let Your Light Shine

Matthew 5:14-16

You are the light of the world. A city that is set on a hill cannot be hidden. Nor do they light a lamp and put it under a basket, but on a lampstand, and it gives light to all who are in the house. Let your light so shine before men, that they may see your good works and glorify your Father in heaven.

"This little light of mine, I'm gonna' let it shine..."

You may remember that song from Sunday school or children's church. It is a simple yet powerful reminder about how God wants us to show up in the world. Light is the natural agent that stimulates sight and makes things visible. Matthew 5:14 tells us, "*WE* are the light of the world." It doesn't say we have to try to be the light, but instead, we <u>are</u> the light. Light is powerful and it removes darkness. When you are the light, it affects everything around you.

OPENLY OBEDIENT

Because we are the light, we have to let our light shine, and help others experience God. We are placed intentionally in certain jobs, conversations, families, situations, etc. to bring light to dark situations. The enemy knows we are the light, and he knows how much power we have to change situations.

You know that job you're saying you can't wait to get away from? You're there for a reason. It's something you have to learn there. You could be there for others to see your actions and win them over for Christ. Someone on that job is dark and it's your assignment to bring light to them. Be patient and pray for guidance and direction. You have to be the light everywhere you are.

You can't hide your light. Once Jesus is in your heart, you can't hide it from anyone. People will see the change in you and know the change is a result of Jesus doing a good work in you. Even when you try to go down an old path, He is right there convicting you telling you to STOP! Think about those things that used to fulfill you and make you happy, but now make you uncomfortable. He is trying to elevate you to another level and He wants others to see what He's doing in you. Keep shining because when others see the change in you, they'll want to know more about your God too.

Faith Lesson:

Shine bright like a diamond.

Today I will...

_____

_____

_____

_____

_____

_____

_____

_____

_____

_____

_____

_____

_____

_____

_____

_____

_____

OPENLY OBEDIENT

20. Sharing is Caring

Mark 16:15

And He said to them, 'Go into all the world and preach the gospel to every creature...'

How could I share all of the good God has done for me without sharing with you how you can get the same relationship? After all, I believe that is the purpose of all my experiences.

God has positioned me to share His gospel with others and it's amazing to be able to explain to people how much He loves us, what He did for us, and what He will continuously do for us. He promised us eternal life, all we have to do is accept His Son Jesus Christ as our Lord and Savior. Receiving Jesus in your heart is one of the best decisions you can ever make and actually the only one you need to make in order to be saved. Romans 10:9 says if you confess with your mouth and believe in your heart that God was raised from the dead, then you will be saved. I pray everyone can experience the Holy Spirit in their bodies and have an encounter with Christ. Your life will be forever changed once Jesus is a part of it.

We are all born sinners, and we have all fallen short. The Bible tells us that the wages of sin is death. Our nature is to sin, but it's only through God sacrificing His son Jesus for us that we receive complete forgiveness. And that's His gift. The gift of God is Eternal Life in Christ Jesus. This is a free gift that He gives us. It's nothing that can be earned or bought. While we were still sinners, He demonstrates how much He loves us by giving His only son to die for us. That is something to shout about! He loves us unconditionally even to the point of death and even when we are at our worst.

You and I can only be saved by confessing our sins and placing our faith in God's Son, Jesus Christ. We must also surrender our lives to Him, letting Him rule in every area of our lives because we now belong to Him. So, simply read this aloud or silently to yourself:

God, I <ins>CONFESS</ins> that I am a sinner and I need Jesus in my life. I <ins>REPENT</ins> of my sins and turn to you. I <ins>BELIEVE</ins> that Jesus is Your son and that He died on the cross for my sins, was buried and He rose from the dead. I <ins>ACCEPT</ins> this by faith. I <ins>INVITE</ins> Jesus to be Lord of my life, to reign and rule in my heart. Thank You, Lord, for forgiving me and saving me.

Guess what? God just heard your prayer. If you prayed this prayer by faith, then welcome to the family of God! The next steps are to spend time daily in prayer and in God's Word. Then, find fellowship with other believers in a church that teaches and preaches the Bible. Most importantly, you should confess Jesus, your Savior, before others. Share your new faith in Christ with your family, coworkers, and others whom God strategically places in your daily path. Continue to be *Openly Obedient* and watch God's blessings flow.

Today I will...

_____

_____

_____

_____

_____

_____

_____

_____

_____

_____

_____

_____

_____

_____

_____

_____

_____

21. Leaving a Legacy

Proverbs 13:22

A Good man leaves an inheritance to his children's children.

I once heard a story about how a simple "hello" stopped someone who was on their way to commit suicide. This man thought he didn't matter and that no one cared about him or noticed him. While walking to the place where he had decided to end his life, he was greeted by a stranger. "Good Morning," this person said. He broke down crying. He cried because no one had said, "Hello" or "Good Morning" to him in a long time. That simple "Good Morning" blocked everything the enemy put into his head to kill, steal, and destroy his life. Something as small as an acknowledgement saved his life.

It makes me think about how I want to be remembered and what I want people to say about me long after I leave this place:

OPENLY OBEDIENT

Janelle Anita Jones was a loving mother, wife, daughter, sister, aunt, niece, granddaughter, cousin, and friend. She brought light wherever she went. She truly cared about people and she showed it every chance she could. She was an inspiration to many and a joy to be around. She took pride in blessing others and putting a smile on their faces. She took her time to get to know people and acknowledged people by their names. Everyone mattered to her. She could go anywhere and someone would know her. She loved meeting new people and learning about their background and upbringing. If she saw someone sitting alone, she would pull up a chair and sit with them. She wanted everyone to be included. She had a way of getting people out of their shell by doing and saying the most random things, but it was her attempt to make everyone comfortable around her. She knew how to "connect" people together. She liked to know everyone because she knew how a stranger could be a blessing, and how she could be a blessing to others. If someone needed anything, Janelle would seek a way to make sure they received it. She never sought out praise for what she did, but she would get an internal happiness in her heart. To know she was able to help one person eat, one person smile, one person feel loved or appreciated meant the world to her. She knew she was being a diligent servant to Christ when she did His work on earth. She was an open book and would share her story with anyone because she never knew who needed to hear it. She was a true Proverbs 31 woman!

Remember her for loving everyone and next time you see a stranger, think of her and just say, "Hello" with a smile. You never know what impact that simple action can have on someone.

Faith Lesson:

Live your life in a way that makes it clear that you were here!

Today I will...

_____

_____

_____

_____

_____

_____

_____

_____

_____

_____

_____

_____

_____

_____

_____

_____

_____

_____

Epilogue

Proverbs 18:22

He who finds a wife, finds a good thing.

Dear You,

I don't know who you are, but I know God will send you to me and we will spend our lives together. I know that our love will represent the love Christ has for the church. I promise to love you unconditionally, be there to lift you up, encourage you, and to never let you fall. I will respect you in private and in public. I promise to bring you good and not harm all the days of my life.

I think about you often, and I can't wait to experience all that God promised me with you. I've been preparing myself for you, and I'm ready to meet you. I took time to make myself whole so when we do meet, we will be two wholes becoming one.

I've been praying specifically for YOU as a person. I know you will be an amazing man with a powerful personality. I pray for your integrity and your honesty. I pray that you stand for what is right. I'm praying for your purpose, hoping that you know why you need me in your life. I want to carry out the purpose God placed in our lives to fulfill together until we meet Him. I'm praying for your past, that you are free from strongholds and "baggage" that will prevent you from being committed to me. I'm praying for your thoughts, hoping that your head is on straight and that you are free from any negative thinking that will hinder your trust when it comes to me. I'm praying for your deliverance, that you are delivered from all addictions that were once a struggle. I cast down any future addictions that will try to entice you. I'm praying for your reputation, hoping that you are well respected and that you are known for being nothing less than a Godly man. I've been praying for your health now and in the future. I pray that God will keep you healthy and free from sickness and diseases. I'm praying for you as a father and protector, hoping that if you are a father now that you have an amazing relationship with the one(s) you brought into the world. If you're not a father, I'm praying that you would be a wonderful father to our children. I pray that you will protect all of us as best as you can. I'm praying for your finances, hoping that you know how to manage your money, that your credit score is excellent, and that you know how to earn money to provide for your family. I'm praying for your self-image, hoping that you see yourself the way God sees you. I hope you love yourself and you take pride in taking care of yourself. But most of all, I'm praying for your relationship with God. I pray that you can already hear His voice and that you fear Him. I pray you're connected to Him and you know deep down that you are nothing without Him. This is so important, because I need you to be led by God so you can lead me. I need to know that you're making Godly decisions so I can confidently submit to you.

I've prepared Dallas for you as well. We have conversations about you often. I want to make sure he knows now that you will love him and that you won't take me away from him. You're an additional person who will love him and care for him. He can't wait to meet you. He said you will have to be nice to me and play video games with him before he agrees to allow you to marry me. I can't wait for you to meet him. You will instantly love him. Just remember it's been the two of us for a while, so be patient with us. We're a dynamic duo and it will be well worth it.

I can't wait to spend the rest of my life with you sleeping beside you and waking up to you. I'm excited to countdown to our yearly anniversaries, to give you a child, and to just be happy with you. I want you to be my purpose partner, fulfilling together, what God has for us.

I will be ready for you when you find me. I know God is preparing me for you, and He will allow us to be together in His perfect timing.

I love you already and I know our love will allow the world to see Christ.

Faith Lesson:

People who get what they want tend to be the ones who make the effort to know what they want. - Martha Beck

Acknowledgements

Rashida McKenzie, I thank God for you. He sent you to help me and guide me. You helped me bring this vision to life. I thank you for your patience with me. I thank you for taking your time to help me put my thoughts together and "dig deeper" when I needed to. Thank you for pushing me and reminding me not to hold back from my testimony because that one thing I left out could potentially help someone out. You made it comfortable for me to share the things I didn't want to share. Thank you for your beautiful spirit. Thank you for your accountability. Thank you for helping me finish my assignment. Thank You for everything. I wish nothing but blessings over you, your family, and your business.

To everyone involved with my book cover:
Snipes Design Agency
Ms. Healthy Hair
Bill Lee Photography
Already Perfect, LLC

Thank You!

Mommy and Daddy, I love you. I hope I continue to make you proud.
To my friends, and family, thank you for loving me and pushing me to be a better me.

About the Author

Janelle Anita Jones is a native of Washington, DC an active member of the First Baptist Church of Glenarden in Upper Marlboro, Maryland, and a Human Resources Professional with the U.S. Federal Government. She is a graduate of North Carolina Agricultural and Technical State University, where she studied Criminal Justice. Janelle has a passion for helping others and leading women to Christ by being a witness to what He has done in her life. Janelle is a proud mother to her eight-year-old son, Dallas.

CONNECT
WITH **JANELLE**

Email: IAmJanelleAnita@gmail.com

Website: www.janelleanita.com

Facebook: Janelle A. Jones

If you enjoyed this book, please write your review on Amazon.com and share it with a friend.